PENPALS for Handwriting

Year 1 Practice Book (5–6 years)

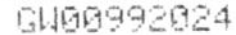

Gill Budgell Kate Ruttle

Series Consultants

Sue Palmer Dr Rhona Stainthorp

Contents

CAMBRIDGE UNIVERSITY PRESS

1 Letter formation practice: long ladder family

Finger trace. Say the sound.

l l l l

Write the letters in your book.

l i l i   j t j t

u i u i   u y u y

Practise the pattern.

Read and write these words.

it

lit

till

Letter formation practice: one-armed robot family

Finger trace. Say the sound.

r r r r

Write the letters and words in your book.

r n m b h k p

pin bun

lip run

Practise the pattern.

Read and write these words.

in

back

him

3 Letter formation practice: curly caterpillar family

Finger trace. Say the sound.

c c c c

Write the letters and words in your book.

o a e s d g q f c

cat dog

fish rat

Practise the pattern.

Read and write these words.

day

get

she

said

Letter formation practice: zig-zag monster family

Finger trace. Say the sound.

z z z z

Write the letters and words in your book.

v v w w x x z z

zebra fox

owl dove

Practise the pattern.

Read and write these words.

very

was

have

5 Practising the vowels: i

Finger trace. Say the sound.

i i i i

Write the letters and words in your book.

i t i p i n i g i

tin

Baked Beans

dig

pip

win

Practise the pattern.

ll= ll= ll= ll=

Read and write these words.

did

will

his

Practising the vowels: u

Finger trace. Say the sound.

u u u u

Write the letters and words in your book.

u n u s u g u h

sun mum

jug hut

Practise the pattern.

Read and write these words.

but

mum

put

Finger trace. Say the sound.

a a a a

Write the letters and words in your book.

a r a b a n

bat tap

rat van

Practise the pattern.

Read and write these words.

had

ran

man

Practising the vowels: *o*

Finger trace. Say the sound.

o o o o

Write the letters and words in your book.

o p o d o g o c

box  dog

mop  cot

Practise the pattern.

Read and write these words.

on

not

got

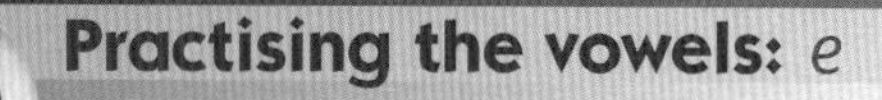

9 Practising the vowels: *e*

Finger trace. Say the sound.

e e e e

Write the letters and phrases in your book.

e n e t e g e p

ten men

ten pegs

Practise the pattern.

lo o lo o lo o

Read and write these words.

yes

get

bed

THE ALPHABET

Write the alphabet in your book.

A B C D E F G

H I J K L M N O P

Q R S T U V W X Y Z

Practise the pattern.

Read and write these words.

OUT

OFF

PULL

PUSH

Introducing diagonal join to ascender: joining *at, all*

Finger trace. Say the sounds.

at all

Write the letters and words in your book.

at at all all

hat fall

bat wall

Practise the pattern.

Read and write these words.

ball

call

that

what

Practising diagonal join to ascender: joining *th*

Finger trace. Say the sound.

th th

Write the letters and the phrase in your book.

th th th th

three thin things

Practise the pattern.

Read and write these words.

them

there

these

Practising diagonal join to ascender: joining *ch*

Finger trace. Say the sound.

ch ch

Write the letters and the phrase in your book.

ch ch ch ch

chicken

and chips

Practise the pattern.

Read and write these words.

chick

chin

much

Practising diagonal join to ascender: joining d

Finger trace. Say the sound.

d d

Write the letters and the phrase in your book.

d d d d

dip dop

to dlass

Practise the pattern.

Read and write these words.

dub

day

dap

Introducing diagonal join, no ascender: joining *in*, *im*

Finger trace. Say the sounds.

in im

Write the letters and words in your book.

in im in im

pin

fin 

Tim 

Kim 

Practise the pattern.

Read and write these words.

bin

him

win

Finger trace. Say the sounds.

cr tr dr

Write the letters and words in your book.

cr cr tr tr dr dr

crown  drink

trip  crab 

Practise the pattern.

lu lu lu lu

Read and write these words.

tree

drum

cross

Practising diagonal join, no ascender: joining *lp*, *mp*

Finger trace. Say the sounds.

lp mp

Write the letters and words in your book.

lp lp mp mp

stamp

gulp

Practise the pattern.

Read and write these words.

help

jump

bump

Introducing diagonal join, no ascender, to an anticlockwise letter: joining *id*, *ig*

Finger trace. Say the sounds.

id ig

Write the letters and the phrases in your book.

id id ig ig

big dig big lid

Practise the pattern.

Read and write these words.

lid

big

hid

19 Practising diagonal join, no ascender, to an anticlockwise letter: joining *nd*, *ld*

Finger trace. Say the sounds.

nd ld

Write the letters and the sentence in your book.

nd nd ld ld

Send me a cold, wild wind.

Practise the pattern.

ccc ccc ccc

Read and write these words.

and

could

old

Practising diagonal join, no ascender, to an anticlockwise letter: joining *ng*

Finger trace. Say the sound.

ng ng

Write the letters and the sentence in your book.

ng ng ng ng

"I'm hungry,"
sang the king.

Practise the pattern.

Read and write these words.

bring

ring

song

Practising diagonal join, no ascender: joining *ee*

Finger trace. Say the sound.

ee ee

Write the letters and the phrase in your book.

ee ee ee ee

three bees on

three trees

Practise the pattern.

eeee eeee

Read and write these words.

been

seen

three

Practising diagonal join, no ascender: joining *ai, ay*

Finger trace. Say the sound.

ai ay

Write the letters and words in your book.

ai ai ay ay

railway

snailway

Practise the pattern.

Read and write these words.

away

again

may

Practising diagonal join, no ascender: joining *ime, ine*

Finger trace. Say the sounds.

ime ine

Write the letters and phrases in your book.

ime ime ine ine

line time

fine time

Practise the pattern.

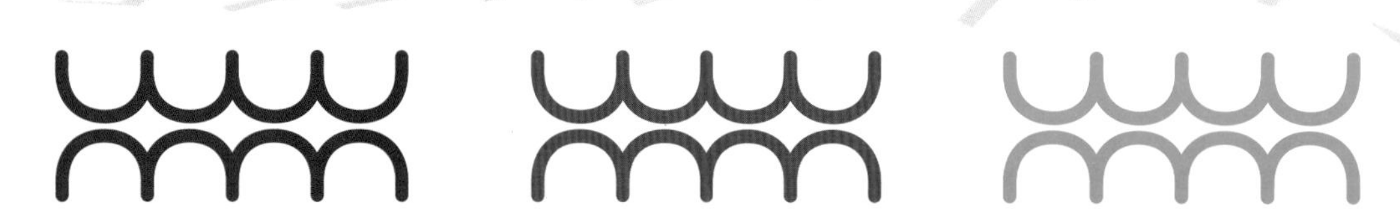

Read and write these words.

nine

time

shine

Introducing horizontal join, no ascender: joining op, oy

Finger trace. Say the sounds.

op oy

Write the letters and words in your book.

op op oy oy

mop hop

boy

ahoy

Practise the pattern.

Read and write these words.

boy

top

hop

toy

Practising horizontal join, no ascender: joining *one, ome*

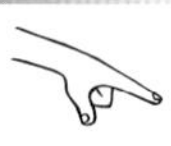

Finger trace. Say the sounds.

one ome

Write the letters and the sentence in your book.

one one ome ome

Come home with the bone.

Practise the pattern.

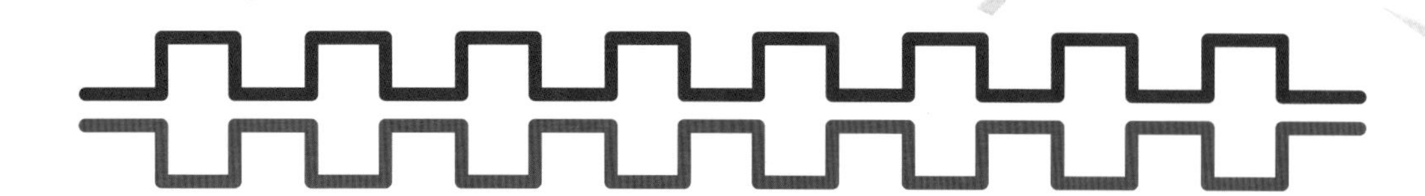

Read and write these words.

home

one

some

Introducing horizontal join, no ascender, to an anticlockwise letter: joining *oa*, *og*

Finger trace. Say the sounds.

oa og

Write the letters and the phrase in your book.

oa oa og og

a frog in a boat

on a moat

Practise the pattern.

Read and write these words.

dog

log

coat

throat

27 Practising horizontal join, no ascender, to an anticlockwise letter: joining *wa, wo*

Finger trace. Say the sounds.

wa wo

Write the letters and the phrase in your book.

wa wa wo wo

two swans

on water

Practise the pattern.

Read and write these words.

want

was

two

would

Introducing horizontal join to ascender: joining ol, ot

Finger trace. Say the sounds.

ol ot

Write the letters and the phrase in your book.

ol ol ot ot

lots of old gold

Practise the pattern.

Read and write these words.

hot

pot

cold

Practising horizontal join to ascender: joining *wh, oh*

Finger trace. Say the sounds.

wh oh

Write the letters and the phrase in your book.

wh wh oh oh

whizzing

wheel

Practise the pattern.

Read and write these words.

when

where

who

30 Introducing horizontal and diagonal joins to ascender, to an anticlockwise letter: joining *of*, *if*

Finger trace. Say the sound.

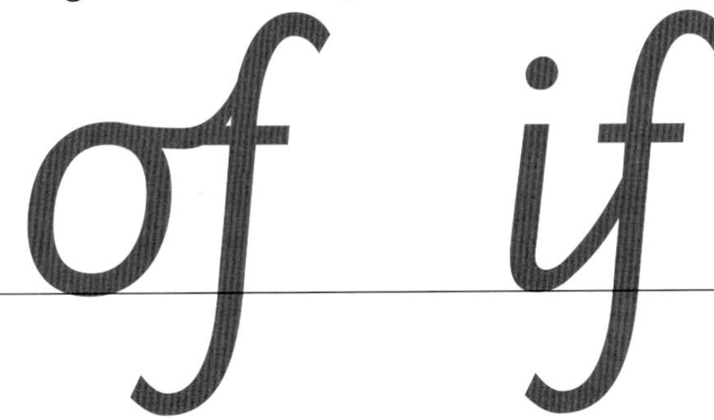

Write the letters and the sentence in your book.

of of if if

I need a lift to my loft.

Practise the pattern.

Read and write these words.

of

if

off

Finger trace. Say the sounds. Write the letters.

all in ig ld

wh og of one

Write the words in your book.

ball win hid held

when bone dog soft

that top dig bid